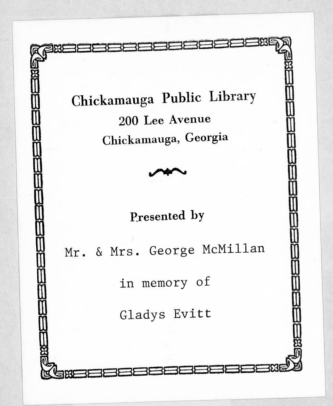

ALL COLOR BOOK OF

ROMAN MYTHOLOGY

BY PETER CROFT

INTRODUCTION BY STEWART PEROWNE

CHARTWELL
BOOKS, INC.

This 1989 edition
published by
Chartwell Books, Inc.
A Division of Book Sales Inc.
110 Enterprise Avenue
Secaucus
New Jersey 07094

© 1974 Octopus Books Ltd

ISBN 1-55521-357-X

Produced by Mandarin Offset
Printed in Hong Kong

CONTENTS

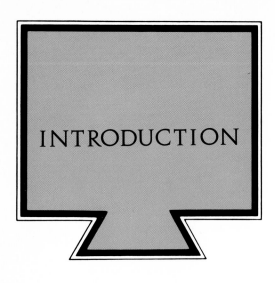

INTRODUCTION

'Ancient Rome' — to us the two words are almost synonymous. When we think of antiquity, it is to Rome that our thoughts automatically turn; and the mere sound of the word Rome is to our ears like the echo of some melancholy passing-bell, tolling for the demise of a glory that is no more.

But the Romans did not think in those terms at all. For them, Rome was forever young and sprightly, 'eternal' in fact, an epithet the Romans themselves applied to their city as early as the latter days of the Republic. They celebrated Rome's birthday every year on the 21st April, as they still do. It is, beyond question, this feeling of eternity which has made, and still keeps, Rome unique. But in Roman eyes, Rome's youth did have one disadvantage: it implied lack of lineage of august ancestry. In the early days this did not matter very much: Rome was just a village, or union of villages, like others, Veii, or Alba Longa or Terracina; but when Rome became a ruling power, first in Italy then beyond its shores and finally the ruling power par excellence, it mattered very much indeed. In particular it mattered in Rome's dealings with three other nations, first the Greeks (and they, be it remembered, included the Greeks of what is now Southern Turkey, 'Asia Minor', one of the most fertile seed-beds of Greek genius), then the Egyptians, who seemed to be older than anyone, certainly older than Homer, and finally the Persians, or Parthians. With the Parthians Rome never came to any amicable understanding, and the fatal antagonism between the two races which lasted until both peoples went down before alien invaders in the seventh century of our era was one of the most destructive oppositions in the whole recorded history of mankind.

With Greece and Egypt relations were easier, if only because they both fell so easily to Roman arms. That made it all the more simple for Rome to appropriate some parts of their religions. It also tells how even from Persia Rome was to import myths, and still more vital how from the apparently negligible strip of land between Persia and Egypt Rome was to attract and assimilate the ideas and aspirations of an unimportant tribe or set of tribes called Hebrews. No one paid much attention to them, but it is worth recording that two of the ablest Romans who ever lived, namely Julius Caesar and Marcus Vipsanius Agrippa, Augustus' prime minister, did.

Mention of Julius Caesar brings us to the core of this book. The Romans are far more of an enigma than the Greeks, though with far fewer variations. We know the exterior features of many more Romans than we do of Greeks. The features of Augustus or of Nero are known to many; but not even the scholars would guarantee to describe just what Pericles or Socrates looked like. On the other hand whereas we know a great deal about the mind of Socrates and the mind of Pericles too, we know very little about how Romans thought; so much so that an English scholar recently told the Classical Association that any two books about Julius Caesar (and he himself has written one of the best) must be books about two different men.

In so far as Caesar was a quintessential Roman, he possessed (besides more questionable qualities) three very Roman attributes: he was proud, prompt and practical. His practicality urged him to some of his most enduring actions, such as the enlargement of the Forum and the reform of the calendar. His promptness has given us two of the best known *mots* of the Roman era. Having divorced his wife, before awaiting the official enquiry into an alleged nocturnal 'scandal' which had occurred in his own official residence, he had dismissed her, he said, because the wife of the High Priest, as he then was, must be above suspicion. That was in 62 BC. Fifteen years later, having conducted a victorious campaign in Asia Minor for a month and seven days he reported his success to the Senate in the immortal words: 'I came, I saw, I conquered — veni, vidi, vici'.

It was Caesar's pride that brought him to his doom; but it was his pride also that made him realize that what Rome needed was a pedigree. Really good mythology, in fact. No, not mythology; let the Greeks have that. Rome would go, and went, one better. 'No one', argued the practical Romans, 'likes being regarded as mythical: everybody is flattered by becoming legendary'. Thus it was that young Julius, when at the age of perhaps 33 he pronounced the funeral oration on his aunt Julia, told his hearers that he was descended on one side from Venus, the patron-goddess of Rome, and on the other from Aeneas, who had founded the city.

In this pronouncement of one of Rome's greatest sons we have the germ of Roman mythology. Both the goddess and the hero were, to put it kindly, obscure.

Obscure they would still be, had it not been for these practical Romans. Venus was really nobody — just a name, like most Roman deities. True, there was a temple down in the Forum to Venus Cloacina, Our Lady of the Sewers, a title which, until recent flights of the French literary genius, must have struck us as odd, the association of love and lavatories is still not regarded as being quite the thing by ordinary people. But Aphrodite! How different is she, the lovely, foam-born goddess, who rose from the azure main near Paphos in Cyprus, and hence was called the Paphian, the Cyprian, the goddess of all things bright and beautiful. Once assimilate Venus with Aphrodite and you have a goddess worth having. As Peter Croft shows us, in comparatively early days all the twelve Roman gods of any consequence had been assimilated to Greek counterparts — all except Apollo, who was so full of grace that no Roman deity could be found to match him, and so he is the only Greek god to retain his Greek name in the Roman pantheon.

Beside the Big Twelve there were as we read in these pages a whole host of godlets, swarms of them, presiding over nearly everything seen or unseen, felt or feared, gods of fertility, of the field, of the hearth, of the boundary, of the door, of the hinges, of the threshold. Gods of fever, gods of rust, gods of sowing, reaping, burning and dung-spreading.

If we ask what comfort these minigods gave to their adepts, the answer is none. They were not meant to. They were intended not to impart solace, but to promote terror. It is hard for us to comprehend how from first to last the Roman mind was saturated with superstition. That primitive Romans should have been afraid of the dark, or of lightning, would not to us seem odd; but what does strike us with bewilderment is that until the very latest days of the pagan Roman world sophisticated gentlemen, cynical authors even, would solemnly insert into a factual narrative such phrases as 'now the portents which foretold the elevation of 'so-and-so' were — anything from a donkey with two heads to a chicken with no liver, a tree withering here, an eagle flying there.

Although we know from Livy, who wrote in the days of Augustus, that in the heyday of the Republic 'enlightened' Romans were tired of all the mumbo jumbo of auspices and entrails, there were many others who went on taking the whole thing seriously. Ovid, the raffish poet who was more interested in earthly bodies than heavenly ones, designed a whole calendar, of which we possess the first six months, telling his smart readers just what must be done on what day, how, where and by whom, to keep Rome in with the gods. This subservience of the proud Romans to superstition makes the Roman quest for *salus*, that is 'health', or salvation all the more engrossing.

The Greeks, despite the Apostle Paul's compliment to the Athenians, were not what we would call a religious people. For them, gods and men were like masters and servants (some gods, such as Heracles and Asclepios, had started below stairs and worked their way up). If you treated them with deference, you could expect decent treatment in return. At least that was the theory, until people like Euripides pointed out that some of the gods were cads. But what did it matter? For the ordinary Hellene the world was full of all sorts of beautiful beings and things, nymphs, dryads, satyrs, Dionysus dispensing wine and ecstasy, mysteries, processions. (Ancient Greece had almost as many 'festivals' as modern Britain.) For more serious folk there was philosophy, the unending search for the temporal answer to the eternal questions. For the Roman there were no such solaces.

Thus it came about that the Romans sought their spiritual comfort elsewhere. First, in their national legends, and that brings us back to Aeneas. The origins of Rome are unexciting but undisputed. Like so many things Roman, the site of Rome was dictated by practical necessity. In the eighth century BC the chief power in northern Italy was the race we know as the Etruscans. We still do not know where they came from, nor, though we admire their arts, can we yet read their language. The river Tiber formed a boundary south of which Latin shepherds and herdsmen lived in humble settlements. The lowest point at which the Tiber was fordable (and the ford itself therefore a danger point for the Latins) was also the first place inland at

This page
A mosaic from Ephesus, Turkey, showing the head of Medusa.

Following page
One of Rome's great spring festivals was the Liberalia, honouring Liber, the god of vine growers, at a time when the latest vintage was ready for drinking. The celebration was common to all wine-producing countries at this season, so Liber came to be identified with the Greek god Dionysus or Bacchus, son of Jupiter and the Theban princess Semele. Bacchus, the name most used by the Romans, was commonly portrayed as in this mosaic from Paphos, Cyprus — a handsome, almost effeminate young man accompanied by a debauched Silenus and seated in a cart drawn by leopards. At the Liberalia Roman youths in their sixteenth year officially came of age and assumed the *toga virilis* — sign of a life free (*libera*) from parental authority.

which the river's southern bank is rendered defensible by two hills, each about 50 metres above sea level, namely the Palatine and the Capitol, as they were afterwards to be known. So it was on these two knolls that Rome came into beginning. Did Romulus exist? He may well have done, even if the wolf is mythical. The story that Cyrus the Persian was suckled by a bitch is no proof that he never lived. So how does Aeneas come in? The answer is the rather surprising one that over a very large part of Italy, that is from Naples southwards, the Greeks had got there long before the Romans. At a time when the inhabitants of Latium were rude goatherds and farmers, standing in awe of their mysterious, cruel but undoubtedly gifted Etruscan neighbours, the Greeks had established colonies imbued with their own civilization on many a smiling site in the south. Clearly therefore, if Rome was to have a respectable ancestry, a Trojan one would be smartest, because whoever may have won the Trojan War, it was obvious that Troy must have been there before the Greeks attacked it, or there would have been no war. (We now know that it was there a very, very long time before.)

So Aeneas, the dutiful son, the single-hearted soldier, this hero-figure becomes the founder of Rome. He is entertained by a shepherd on the Palatine. The shepherd is Evander, himself of Trojan origin. Thus is Rome's pedigree fabricated and authenticated.

Although Rome was now respectable, Rome was far from being religious, as we understand the term. True, on the Capitol there presided the Great Triad, Jupiter, Juno, assimilated with Hera, the wife of Zeus, and Minerva assimilated with Athena. Venerated here and there in the city below were the other minor, but still important, deities already mentioned. The Roman's relationship with them was, as already said, one of propitiatory dread. 'My will be done' was the Roman's attitude to religion and to those by whose means the gods might be wheedled into granting that will, even towards such sacrosanct Cinderellas as the Vestal Virgins, or the great Flamen Dialis, hedged about with so many cramping taboos that the office might remain vacant for years for lack of a candidate. The real bankruptcy of Roman ideas of deity was apparent to one and all when it became the custom (borrowed from the east) to 'deify' emperors. Augustus and Tiberius resisted it as far as they could, but the practice soon became established. It used to puzzle and shock Victorian moralists, because they unwittingly compared Roman concepts of godhead with their own; but the idea of a sublime, ineffable God was quite alien to Roman thought, as it was — again we turn to Paul's experience at Athens — to most of the Greeks as well. The word *divus* as applied posthumously to an emperor meant no more than the epithet 'most sacred' as applied to Hanoverian majesty, if as much.

Which brings us to the supreme interest and significance of Roman mythology, its importations from abroad. As will be seen from this book, these importations fall into three categories: philosophy, 'mystery' cults and monotheism. Of the philosophies, the two most important systems were those of the Epicureans and the Stoics. Both had started, almost simultaneously, in post-Alexandrine Athens, as manifestations of man's concern for himself as an *individual* not merely as a civic unit. Both set out to achieve *salus*, that is 'health' meaning spiritual health, but the methods that they advocated were very different. Whereas the Epicurean sought to dissociate himself from the world and all things worldly, the Stoic taught that there is a Providence which is active in the world, and that it is man's stern duty to conform to the ordinances of this deity. This idea is not Greek at all, because the founder of Stoicism was not a Greek, but a Semite called Zeno, from Kitium in Cyprus. Thus we have in Stoicism the first and vital contact with the Semitic concept of the sublime, which was to be more mightily developed first in Judaism and then in Christianity.

Next come the foreign deities, the exotics from Asia and Egypt. The first alien deity to enter Rome was, as Peter Croft shows, Cybele, the Great Mother from Asia; and how strange was her advent, as a talisman against Rome's great enemy, Hannibal, and a successful talisman too. After her the gods of Asia arrive in an ever-increasing company. Then come the Egyptians, Isis in particular and Sarapis. These deities had the double advantage of being extremely ancient and also of inhabiting splendid and famous shrines in their unique homeland, where a bountiful river nourished mankind in a manner unparalleled in any other region of the known world. From time to time these alien cults caused scandals and were 'banished', but such was the solace (and excitement) they provided, so utter was their contrast with the dry-as-dust exercises of the indigenous religion, that they always made their way back, and rekindled their affecting liturgies. They were indeed what Milton rebukingly called them: 'gay religions, full of pomp and gold'.

Once the procession had started, it moved with ever-increasing impetus, if only because Roman arms and Roman policy brought Rome into contact with so many exotic cults. As this book makes clear, there was as yet no sense of coercion in religions: you simply chose the one, or ones, which you felt would give you most comfort. Another point must be made — very few of the foreign liturgies prescribed a code of conduct. Stoicism did; and we must now mention three others which were in accord with Matthew Arnold's cardinal dictum that 'conduct is three-fourths of life', and they will lead us naturally to the third and most fruitful external graft onto the gnarled trunk of Roman religion, that is, monotheism. First and foremost comes Mithraism. Thanks to the great Belgian scholar Franz Cumont, we are now able to make a fairly accurate estimate, admirably mirrored in Dr Croft's pages, of the great influence which Mithras exercised throughout the empire. The vestiges of a Mithraum are still visible in the City of London; and as if to show how eclectic Roman religion was, this same shrine has yielded the finest head of Sarapis in existence. The heads of both gods from this site are now in the Guildhall Museum. There was at one time a tendency to overestimate the influence of Mithraism. 'If', says Renan, in his *Marc-Aurèle*, 'Christianity had been arrested in its growth by some mortal malady, the world would have been Mithraist'. Few would agree with that verdict today, but that Mithraism did bestow a real spiritual elevation, by imposing a real moral discipline, upon Roman belief and practice is undoubted.

Mithras was intimately associated with the sun. Sun-worship is an ancient rite. (It survives to this day in pagan manifestations of varying silliness on every available *plage*, with the accompaniment of the reintroduced burnt sacrifice of human flesh.) The Romans were first introduced to the sun cult in the days of Augustus, when that astute psychologist, as part of his campaign to rejuvenate Rome, imported the most ancient religious symbols then known — far older than anything those Greeks could produce — namely, two obelisks from Egypt. They were the first of the thirteen which now adorn the city. One, originally quarried at Aswan between 1232 and 1200 BC, now stands in the Piazza del Popolo, the other, dating from the early years of the sixth century BC, on Montecitorio. Both are inscribed by their imperial donor as 'gifts to the sun' — correctly enough, because as Pliny knew, obelisks were regarded by the Egyptians as symbolizing the sun's rays. Augustus had imported them for political reasons; but by introducing these 'gifts to the sun' he was in fact preparing the way for the worship of the 'Unconquered Sun'. After the marriage of the Emperor Septimius Severus to Julia Domna, the daughter of the priest of the sun god at Emesa, this was to become increasingly fashionable in Rome, until by the end of the third century it was established as to all intents and purposes the official state religion. Augustus of course, could not have foreseen this, nor would he have approved of it. His aim was to revivify the old Roman religion, the 'gods of earth and altar' so touchingly portrayed on his Altar of Peace, itself one of the most moving religious sculptures ever created. Then, too, Augustus had at his service one of the most spiritually minded poets who ever sang, namely Virgil. It is largely due to the Augustan policy of 'renewal' that the old Roman religion did contrive to survive for so long. With the sun, monotheism had come to Rome, and so would ultimately make it the hearth and centre as it still is of a monotheistic faith which for 300 years Rome did all in her power to eradicate, namely Christianity.

The Christian Faith sprang from a Jewish matrix. Exactly when the Jews reached Rome it is not possible to say. That they were 'expelled' from the city in 139 BC we do know. By the end of the Republican period they were a numerous community, and a very valuable one. The Jews were not only worshippers of a single God, but they claimed that He was the One and Only God, and that all men ought to obey his commands, led and enlightened by His chosen servants. Here was something entirely novel in religious experience. It was naturally unpopular in easy-going pagan circles, but it did stand up to practical tests. These Jews, with their strict rules of conduct —

the Ten Commandments they called them — supplemented by practical regulations for the living of everyday life, including honesty in commerce, really were more trustworthy than many a loose-living Gentile. It therefore happened that while their exclusiveness made them unpopular as it has often done since, their standards and methods made them respected by those whose respect was worth having, as it still does. Not all those who admired them joined their community; but they emulated their precepts.

From among such folk there finally appeared what was at first regarded as a mere 'splinter-group' of Judaism. Soon however it became clear that the Christians were nothing of the sort; they claimed to be the apostles of an universal Faith, nay more, of the universal Faith. This brought upon them violent antagonism, first from the Jews, who regarded the Christians both as blasphemers (for exalting a man to Godhead) and as renegades (for proclaiming that the spiritual patrimony of Jewry might be appropriated by any who cared to partake of it), and then from the Romans, who regarded 'King Jesus' as a subversive rival.

Thus was played out the long, triumphant tragedy. In the end, it was both Caesar and Christ who were the victors, aided not a little by the Unconquered Sun, who had done so much to shed the light of Salvation amid the family of the first Christian emperor, Constantine.

Peter Croft has undertaken to retell this fascinating story. It is not only fascinating, but in fact timely. The subject which his book expounds is the evolution of Roman religion from a hut on the Palatine to the Basilica of Saint Peter's from the Forum to the ends of the earth. The foundation, in fact, of the era of European civilization which is now drawing to a close. (No era ever thinks it will draw to a close, but they all do.) What is to succeed it we still cannot discern. It is all the more necessary therefore to have a sure grasp of our own civilization as we possess it.

Stewart Perowne

GENVS · VNDE
LATINVM

BEFORE THE DAWN

CHAPTER I

The Romans' firm belief that they were of Trojan origin was based on the myth of Aeneas, the son of an otherwise obscure Trojan prince, Anchises, and the goddess of love, Venus. Such unions were not unknown in the histories of aristocratic families, and the Julians, represented by such men of distinction as Julius Caesar and his great-nephew Augustus, claimed that their *gens* or clan was descended directly from Aeneas himself. In this fresco from Rome's Palazzo Farnese the consummation of Venus's love for Anchises is vividly portrayed by Caracci and neatly expressed in the words of the poet Virgil — *genus unde Latinum* — 'the origins of the Romans'.

Above

Troy stands on the narrow strip of water that forms the barrier between Greece and Turkey. On these plains, seen here from the crumbling remains of the once-proud city, was fought the famous war between the Greeks and the Trojans, ostensibly over the rape of Helen, a Greek queen, by the Trojan prince Paris. Paris had been granted this privilege by Venus when he awarded her the golden apple as a prize for beauty in a competition held on Mount Ida. By doing so Paris inevitably incurred the displeasure of the other two contestants, Juno, the queen of the gods, and Minerva, or Athene, as the Greeks called her, who arranged for him to be killed in the war.

Right

The Trojan War continued indecisively for ten years and was eventually ended by a Greek trick, the Wooden Horse. The Horse, with Greek soldiers in its belly, was left on the plains of Troy while the rest of the Greeks sailed away — to return the next night after the Trojans had been tricked by a Greek confidence man into thinking that the Horse would protect Troy if it were taken inside the city. It was, and the Greeks inside it let themselves out in the darkness and opened the gates of Troy to their returning forces. This wall painting from Pompeii shows the Horse being brought into the city amid excited crowds.

Below

Episodes from the sack of Troy are depicted on this marble relief of the first century AD found at Bovillae near Albano in Italy, now in the Capitoline Museum at Rome. The inscription tells us that the scenes are taken from a work (now lost) of Stesichorus, a lyric poet who flourished in Sicily in the sixth century BC. One scene shows Aeneas with Ascanias and Anchises and bears the legend 'Aeneas setting out for the Western Land with his family'. From this it has been inferred that the myth of Aeneas's migration to Italy goes back at least to the time of Stesichorus. But this has been doubted by recent scholars.

Right

Troy has been destroyed. Aeneas has been saved by his mother Venus, who has told him that he must leave Troy and found another city overseas. In this splendid marble group, now in the Borghese Gallery at Rome, Bernini has portrayed the piety of Aeneas, who carries on his shoulders his aged father, paralyzed by Jupiter in revenge for his affair with Venus. In his emaciated hands Anchises supports the symbols of Troy, the Penates or household gods. Behind them stumbles the young Ascanias, carrying a torch not only to illuminate his father's path but also to ensure the continuity of the spirit of Troy.

Left

The sun breaks through storm clouds over the bay of Carthage to bathe the ruined columns of the Roman city. Carthage was originally founded as a Phoenician colony and trading post on the North African coast, near what is now Tunis. Here Aeneas and the survivors of the Trojan War landed in their quest for a new homeland, after being blown off course by a storm prompted by Juno, who was determined to destroy the last vestiges of a race she hated. But Destiny decreed otherwise. Carthage, a city dedicated to Juno, was fated to be destroyed by the heirs of Aeneas. In fact, the city was totally razed by Rome after a triple series of wars, the most famous of which is for ever associated with Hannibal.

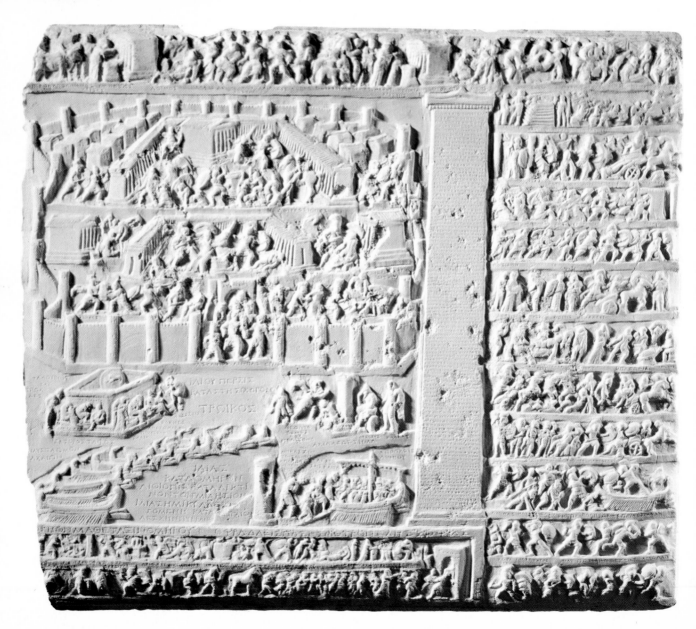

Left
This is an illustration from the *Codex Romanus*, a manuscript written in the fifth or sixth century AD, now in the Vatican Library. Textually, perhaps, it is less than accurate, but visually it is one of the most attractive of the editions of Virgil's *Aeneid*. The ships of Aeneas are tossed by a storm, personified by the malignant figures above them, while the hero raises pious hands to pray that he should not suffer such an ignominious death. The crews seem splendidly placid amid the tumoil around them, and the presence of the sea monsters waiting with beady eyes for their prey — in vain. Neptune came to the rescue and calmed his se

Below
Aeneas is welcomed to Carthage by Queen Dido outside the Temple of Juno. He is attended by his faithful companion, Achates. The pair had set out, after their two ships reached land safely, to explore and find the rest of their comrades who had been dispersed by the storm in the fleet's other five ships. While searching they met Venus, disguised as a huntress (centre), and she not only soothed their anxieties but told them where they were and some essential facts about Dido. In this illumination from a manuscript in the

British Museum, Venus points heavenwards to seven swans, symbols of Aeneas's seven ships. The other five are shown sailing safely into the harbour at rear.

Above
This mosaic now in the British Museum delightfully epitomizes the legend of Aeneas and Dido, a hesitant man and a determined woman. Aeneas had left Troy seven years before. He was weary and often despaired of fulfilling his destiny, the founding of a new Troy. He had been received in Carthage with enthusiasm by its queen and the temptation to linger was great — too great to resist. He was flattered, too, by the attention Dido showed him, an attention which turned to admiration, love, and eventually to an unconquerable passion. The hunt shown here provided the climax of the story.

Right
The act of consummation. During the hunt Dido and Aeneas shelter in a cave from a storm. The whole episode was engineered by Juno and Venus from different motives of hate and affection. As Virgil graphically wrote, 'The sky connived at the union, the lightning flared, on their mountain peak nymphs raised their cry. On that day were sown the seeds of suffering and death'. The news spread and Aeneas was recalled to his destiny by Jupiter, who sent his messenger Mercury with a curt reminder. This illustration is also to be found in the *Codex Romanus*.

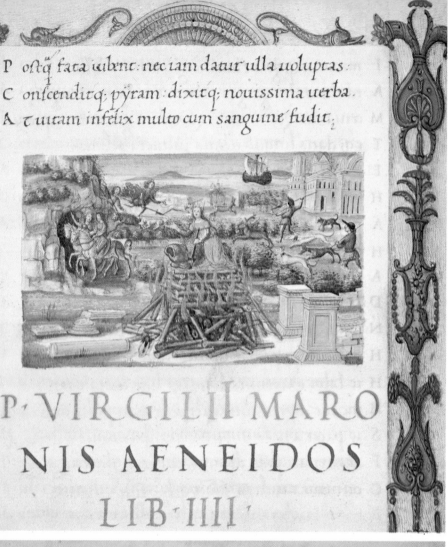

P ostq̃ fata iubent: nec iam datur ulla uoluptas.

C onscenditq; pyram: dixitq; nouissima uerba.

A t uitam infelix multo cum sanguine fudit.

P· VIRGILII MARO

NIS AENEIDOS

LIB· IIII·

TEMPLVMAPOLLINIS

ACHATES · AENEAS · SIBYLLA

Left

The final scene in the story of Dido's love for Aeneas was her death by her own hand. On this exquisite page at the beginning of Book IV of the *Aeneid* the scribe has painted both the beginning and end of this tragedy, the entry into the cave during the hunt and the suicide on the funeral pyre. The events in between are poignantly told by Virgil: how love turned to passion, despair, and ultimately hate, while Dido tried to stop Aeneas from leaving her. As one modern commentator has written, 'The story of Dido has haunted the imagination of Europe, drawing tears from saints and sinners, from St Augustine in the fourth century as from Anatole France in the twentieth'.

Right

This painting from Modena by a minor Renaissance artist ingeniously presents the events of the whole of Book V of the *Aeneid*, 871 lines of poetry. It depicts the return of Aeneas to Sicily after leaving Carthage, an interval of calm between the tragedy of Dido's suicide, still unknown to Aeneas, and the hero's dramatic descent to the Underworld. In the centre games are held near Anchises' tomb, on the anniversary of his death at Drepanum in the north of Sicily: sailing and foot races, boxing and archery, followed by an equestrian exercise of young men. In the background a snake glides from the tomb, where it consumes the sacrifices, an omen of dubious significance. Iris ascends her rainbow after persuading the Trojan women to burn their fleet and end their wanderings. They are thwarted (foreground), and Venus asks Neptune to give her son a safe voyage to Italy, which is marred only by the loss of the helmsman, Palinurus, seen tumbling overboard, an innocent victim to placate the sea god. Dominating the whole is a sugar-cake Segesta, the city Aeneas founded in Sicily.

Left

Aeneas has landed in Italy at Cumae near Naples to seek the aid of the Sibyl, Apollo's priestess and prophetess, for his promised journey into Hades, the land of the dead. Achates again accompanies his leader, and the Sibyl, less frenzied than Virgil describes her, carries a branch in her hand, because she usually wrote her prophecies on leaves which were scattered by winds through her cave. The temple at rear belies Virgil's account of a vast cave as the Sibyl's seat. But excavations at Cumae have revealed a long gallery ending in a large chamber similar to the galleries of Tiryns and Mycenae in Greece – a clear link with a Trojan past.

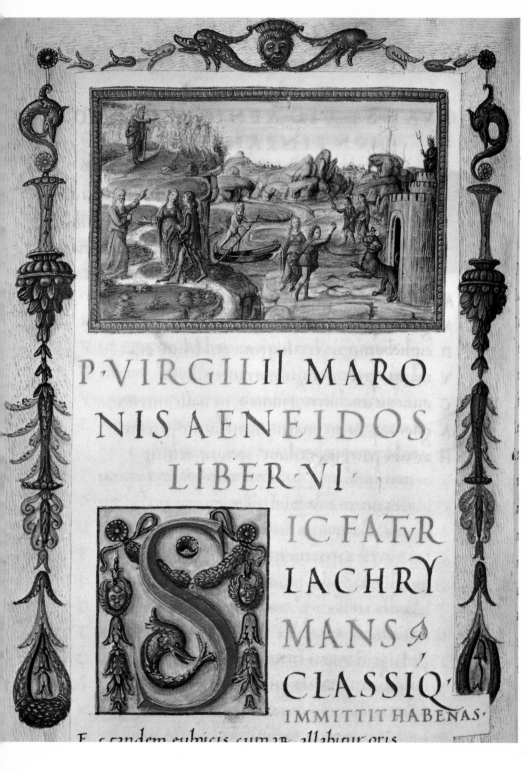

P·VIRGILII MARO
NIS AENEIDOS
LIBER·VI·
IC FATvR
IACHRY
MANS
CLASSIQ'
IMMITTIT HABENAS·

Above
Aeneas sets off for the Underworld with the Sibyl, who acts as guide, having had the advantage of a previous trip. Charon ferries them across the Styx, the river which separates this world from the next, although their weight almost sinks a boat accustomed to hold insubstantial phantoms. Once across, they face the three-headed dog, Cerberus, who guards the entrance to Hades, and pacify him with drugs. Eventually they reach the Elysian Fields, where Anchises carries out his task of revealing the future to his son.

Here he points out the souls of future Romans destined to achieve fame in their country's service, an opportunity for Virgil to aid his emperor's propaganda about the greatness of Rome.
Right
The Temple of Mars Ultor, the avenging god of war (centre) was built by Augustus to fulfil a vow made before his victory at Philippi over the murderers of his kinsman and predecessor Julius Caesar. An open space or forum surrounded the temple, which contained statues of Mars and Venus as well as an object of special

veneration, Caesar's own sword. In this way Augustus contrived to remind his countrymen of the two legends about Rome's origins: that the Julian *gens* was descended from Venus through Aeneas, and that Mars was the father of the twins, Romulus and Remus, who founded a city on the site of Rome.

Above

The last six books of Virgil's epic describe Aeneas's difficuities and ultimate success in founding a colony in Latium in Italy. But although he was received kindly on arrival by Latinus, king of the Latins, the prospect of the new colony was unwelcome to Latinus's neighbours, and when the king offered Aeneas the hand of his only child, Lavinia, in marriage, this was too much for Turnus, the prince to whom she was already betrothed. War was inevitable, but Aeneas found an unexpected ally in Evander, a Greek who had recently settled on the future site of Rome and was hard pressed by the same enemies. On the left Venus arms Aeneas with new weapons especially made for him by Vulcan. On the right Evander welcomes Aeneas from his ship.

Following page

The site of Lavinium, Aeneas's colony, was revealed to him in a dream by the river god Tiber, who told him to claim the spot where he found a white sow with a litter of thirty young. In this marble relief Aeneas, still accompanied by Achates, is about to sacrifice the sow to Juno, who had tried in vain to stop his arrival in Italy. In the shrine behind him are the household gods, the Penates, which Aeneas had brought from Troy. The relief is from the Ara Pacis Augustae in Rome.

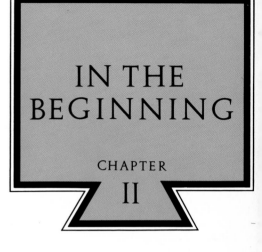

IN THE BEGINNING

CHAPTER
II

The father of Romulus and Remus was
Mars and their mother was Rhea Silvia, a
princess of Alba Longa, a city which was
settled from Lavinium by Ascanias,
Aeneas's son. Numitor, the king of Alba,
was expelled by his younger brother,
Amulius, who butchered his nephews and
made his niece Rhea Silvia a Vestal
Virgin, ostensibly to honour her but in
fact to stop her having any children. The
precaution was useless because she was
made pregnant by Mars. When her twins
were born, the king ordered them to be
thrown into the Tiber. But the Tiber was
in flood, the babies' basket floated, and
when the water subsided the twins were
left in the reeds, where they were found
and suckled by a wolf. These incidents
are portrayed on this ancient altar.

Above left
The Flemish artist Rubens has depicted the moment when Romulus and Remus are discovered by the king's herdsman, Faustulus, while the river god leans against the source of the Tiber, accompanied by a demurely seventeenth-century nymph. The tree in the foreground is a fig – Rubens knew his mythology! Faustulus gave the boys to his wife, Larentia, to nurse. The name Larentia is assumed to mean the mother of the Lares, the deified ancestors and guardian gods of a community. Romulus and Remus were the ancestors of the Roman people and so on their death became Lares. The boys grew up to lead their fellows in several escapades which came to the attention of their grandfather, Numitor. Amulius was killed, the people of Alba told the true facts, and Numitor restored to his throne.

Left
This splendid bronze of the wolf which suckled Romulus and Remus is now appropriately housed on the Capitoline Hill, the centre of Rome. In fact the wolf is antique, an Etruscan work of the fifth century BC, and the twins were made by a fifteenth-century Florentine artist, Pollaiuolo. The Roman historian Livy tells us that the wolf suckled them on the spot by the River Tiber where she found them, which was later marked by a fig tree, the ficus Ruminalis. The goddess Rumina was a primeval goddess of nursing whose name is said to be connected with *ruma*, 'a breast'. The exposure of the twins sounds suspiciously like the early history of Cyrus, king of Persia, or the myth of Neleus and Pelias, twin sons of Poseidon, who were suckled respectively by a bitch and a mare. It is a neat way of accounting for the arrival of a new force lacking background or family.

Above
Hercules, shown here in a Roman statue from Manisa, in present-day Turkey, featured early in Rome's history. As one of his twelve Labours Hercules had to fetch the cattle of Geryon from the west and bring them back to Greece. He paused at the Tiber on his way and while he was asleep a local giant named Cacus stole some of the cows. Hercules managed to recover them and killed Cacus with his club. Recognizing the hero, Evander, the Greek who was the site's first colonist, hailed him as a god. Hercules promptly built himself an altar – the Ara Maxima – and sacrificed one of Geryon's cattle.

Above right
The River Tiber played a big part in the legends of early Rome. As a result of its association with the miraculous survival of Romulus and Remus the neighbouring hills were chosen for the first Roman settlements. The most famous legend connected with the river is that of Horatius Cocles, who with two companions faced the entire Etruscan army on the one bridge left across the Tiber until it was destroyed in his rear, a legend immortalized in Macaulay's *Lays of Ancient Rome*. The Ponte Sant'Angelo here shown was originally built by the Emperor Hadrian and later decorated with statues of angels by Bernini.

Following pages
Romulus found difficulty in populating his new settlement of Rome, particularly because of a shortage of women. He therefore invited the neighbouring tribe of the Sabines to a festival, and at a given signal the young women spectators were seized. Panic was followed by bitter fighting between Romans and Sabines. The battle was finally brought to an end by the intervention of the women. Sabine by birth and Roman by marriage, they naturally considered stalemate better than victory by either side. In this picture the French artist David has shown little historical knowledge, but that may have been what his public expected and liked.

Above

Castor and Pollux, seen here in mosaics
from Paphos in Cyprus, were the twin
sons of Leda and Jupiter – and known
as Dioscuri by the Greeks. Traditionally,
they made their first appearance on the
Roman scene in 496 BC. The Romans
were at war with the Latins, who were
supporting the Tarquins, the deposed
kings of Rome, in their effort to regain
power. The two armies met in battle at
Lake Regillus near Tusculum and in the
course of the equally matched engagement
the Roman commander, Postumius,
secured Castor's help by vowing to build
a temple to him if he were successful. It
was commonly believed that both Castor
and Pollux had fought for the Romans
and afterwards brought news of the
victory to Rome. The brothers also
apparently assisted at subsequent Roman
battles. In later times they were identified
with the constellation Gemini by the
Roman poet Ovid.

Below

The statue of the dying Gaul, now in the
Capitoline Museum in Rome, recalls the
invasions into central Italy by the Gauls
in the fourth century BC. As they swept
south from the Anio, Rome was in peril,
and tradition has it that only the cackling
of the sacred geese saved the Capitoline
Hill from capture. The legends are
preserved in Livy's *History* and
archaeologists confirm
the occupation.

Left
The Forum at Rome was not only the
political centre of the city, but also the
scene of many of the early myths
unfolded in this book. Across it and up
to the Capitoline Hill ran the main street,
the Via Sacra. In the foreground are the
three columns of the Temple of the
Dioscuri and the remains of the tiny
Temple of Vesta. The three Corinthian
columns on a massive podium (right)
are all that is left of the Temple of
Castor and Pollux, rebuilt and dedicated
in 6 AD by Tiberius, the heir apparent
of the reigning Emperor Augustus. The
temple was on the site of the original
building vowed by Postumius at the
Battle of Lake Regillus and dedicated
by his son, Livy tells us, on 15th July,
484 BC, the anniversary of the
engagement. The temple was built on
this site because it was next to the spring
— the Lacus Juturnae — where
traditionally Castor and Pollux were
seen watering their horses after bringing
the news of the battle to Rome. The
open space beyond is the area of the
Lacus Curtius, in early times a marsh
though dry by the time of Augustus.
According to one legend, the Sabine
leader Mettius Curtius rode his horse
into this swamp while being pursued by
the Romans, but managed to escape.

Left
The incident depicted in this picture by
the fifteenth-century artist Domenico
Morone occurred in the same year,
508 BC, as Horatius's defence of the
bridge, and concerned the same enemy,
who were now besieging Rome. Gaius
Mucius, a young aristocrat, volunteered
to enter the Etruscan camp and
assassinate Lars Porsenna, their king.
Unfortunately, he attacked the wrong
man, a secretary, who was sitting by the
king. Taken prisoner, Mucius thrust his
right hand into the fire burning on a
nearby altar, to show the king his
disregard of physical pain. Impressed,
the king released him and, through fear
of similar attempts on his life, negotiated
peace with the Romans. In this way
Mucius earned the nickname of Scaevola
or Left-Handed, the name of a family
distinguished in later Roman history.

CVMAEA

Left

The Sibyl of Cumae played a significant part in the myths of Rome. Michelangelo immortalized her on the ceiling of the Sistine Chapel, here, as a pagan prophetess, who with her sisters balances the Old Testament prophets and reminds the popes of the fusion of the two cultures in Christianity. It was the Sibyl who brought to Tarquinius Superbus, Rome's last king, those invaluable books of prophecy which at first he refused on economic grounds. Eventually he was persuaded by an unusual sales technique into purchasing the last three books for the price of the original nine, after the Sibyl had burnt the other six. They were carefully preserved and consulted on historic occasions.

This page

Saturnus was by origin and doubtful definition an Italian god of agriculture who had lived on earth as a king in Italy, presiding over a Golden Age. He later came to be identified as Time, in which guise he appears here, with his wheel and a child in his lap representing the New Year, in the fourteenth-century campanile of the Cathedral in Florence. He was also identified with the Greek Cronus, father of Jupiter, who overthrew him and usurped his power. His chief festival was the Saturnalia, which began on 17th December each year and in its riotous licence bore some resemblance to the less religious side of our Christmas festivities.

Left

The Roman Forum is seen at dawn. In the foreground are the eight Ionic columns of the Temple of Saturnus standing high above vaults where the bronze money of the senatorial treasury was stored — the Romans frequently used their temples for more than religious purposes. This temple stood at the foot of the Capitol and so symbolized, if not deliberately, the subservience of the old order of Saturnus to that of Jupiter whose imposing temple stood on the Capitol. The present columns belong to a reconstruction of the fourth century AD but tradition says that the earliest Temple of Saturnus was built in 497 BC on the site of an even more ancient altar to the god.

Right

The legends of the Greek Pan, spirit of the mountains and woods, are numerous. Known to the Romans as Faunus, he retained the lecherous qualities of Pan, symbolized by his lower half being that of a goat, as in this mosaic from Paphos. In his honour was held annually the Lupercalia, most primitive of Roman rituals. Aristocratic youths ran naked up and down the Via Sacra, striking bystanders with strips of goatskins. Later the ceremony changed character until it came to be thought of as a fertility rite, but it is probable that they were originally impersonating wolves — *lupi* — menacing Rome's flocks.

Left

Pompeii was a sophisticated urban society in 79 AD when the city was destroyed by the eruption of Mount Vesuvius. Among evidence of this revealed by excavations is a vivid bronze of Faunus that occupied a prominent position in what was the *atrium* of a well-to-do family's house. The original statue is now in the Naples Museum; this modern cast has been placed on the original spot. If the proximity of Vesuvius constantly reminded the Pompeians of primitive forces better recognized than ignored, no god could have been more evocative of this than Faunus.

Above

Portunus, the god of communications, was an ancient Latin god. Virgil represents him in the Sicilian games instituted by Aeneas as giving one of the ships a helping hand. He seems to have been considered variously as god of the harbour – *portus* – or of the gate – *porta*. The latter has caused some confusion with Janus, god of doorways. A festival in his honour – the Portunalia – was held annually in August on the anniversary of the dedication of his temple. This building may or may not have been Portunus's temple, but it does stand where one Roman author tells us his temple stood, near the Aemilian Bridge, beside the Tiber. It is one of the few pre-Augustan buildings in Rome to be well preserved.

Right and above

In the centre of a primitive house was the hearth, where a fire was kept burning for cooking and warmth. Like water and air, fire was a symbol of life, and it inspired the cult of Vesta, introduced to Rome by Numa. Vesta's temples were usually round, symbolizing the hearth they embraced, like this one (above), which is at Tivoli, not far from Rome, situated high above the River Anio. Ovid tells us that Vesta was the daughter of Saturnus and Ops, goddess of the harvest. She was a virgin, as were her ministers, six young women of aristocratic birth who tended the sacred flame. Vesta's temple in Rome was built next to the Regia, traditional

home of the king as chief priest or Pontifex Maximus (left). These graceful columns and part of the wall are all that remain in the Forum of a later restoration, dominated by the eastern side of the Palatine Hill, visible in the background.

Right
Janus was a unique god who appeared only in Roman mythology. As god of doorways, he faced both outwards and inwards, and was therefore commonly depicted with two heads, as on this coin. Janus was also the god of beginnings and gave his name to the first month of each year. In addition, the first day of every month was sacred to him. His cult was established when Numa, the second king of Rome, built him a temple near the Senate House in the Forum. In times of war its gates were always left open, and so turbulent was Rome's history that Livy records only three occasions on which they were closed.

Above

The Lares were the twin sons of Mercury
and the nymph Lara, and as Mercury was
the protector of travellers it was natural
to find shrines to his sons at crossroads,
those places of vital decision for the
traveller. In addition, a small shrine or
Lararium usually graced a Roman house.
The one here, found at Pompeii, shows
the two Lares dancing, with upheld
drinking horns. The snake beneath may
symbolize the spirit of the dead.

Left
Rivers in Italy are usually powerful
forces, especially in spring after the
winter snows have melted; no wonder,
then, that they were deified. At Rome the
River Tiber was annually placated on
14th May when *argei* — bundles of rushes
resembling men bound hand and foot —
were carried to the river by priests called
pontifices, 'bridge builders', whose task
must originally have been to appease the
river when a bridge was thrown over it,
rendering it inferior to man. This statue
represents another river god, the Nile, as
is clear from the sphinx on which he

reclines; it is in the piazza of the Capitol.

Above
If rivers could be represented as gods,
why not towns and countries? Temples
were built to Rome as a goddess, and
she was often associated with the emperor
himself. This mosaic from a villa at
Piazza Armerina in central Sicily portrays
Africa as a handsome woman. Surrounded
by her animals, including the mythical
phoenix (left), she holds in her left arm
a horn, symbol of plenty, taken from an
elephant, while her right hand clasps a
palm tree.

Following pages
The Roman instinct for seeing divinity in
nature is beautifully expressed in this
relief of Earth personified as a mature but
graceful mother with twins on her knee.
The babies may represent Romulus and
Remus, for the relief comes from the
Altar of Peace — the Ara Pacis —
dedicated by Augustus to herald the
end of wars throughout the Roman
Empire. The relief is embellished with
plants and flowers and other signs of
the earth's fruitfulness, and air and
water are also personified, in the sea
serpent and the swan.

Left and right

The Romans were an earthy people, with many agricultural divinities. Pomona, the goddess of fruit trees, was important enough to have her own priests, *flamines*; the two Pales were deities of stock breeding. There were Consus and Ops, gods of storing away and plenty; Flora, who saw to the flowering of crops, was saluted at a festival of games, the Ludi Florales, each April. And Robigus, god of rust, brought mildew to crops if not appeased with a sacrifice of a sheep and a dog. These two pictures illustrate the personification which with the Romans was the first step to deification. One is a fresco of Spring from a villa wall in Stabiae *right*; the other, from a Cyprus house, is a mosaic of fruitful Autumn *left*.

Below left

At Praeneste, in the hills southeast of Rome, there still stands the terrace of the famous shrine and oracle of the goddess Fortuna. It was probably from here that her cult was introduced into Rome by King Servius Tullius. She had no festival but several shrines under various titles, such as Virilis, or Muliebris — of men, or of women. One such shrine, Livy records, was built to commemorate the time in 488 BC when the traitor Coriolanus was persuaded by his wife and mother to lead away the army which he had brought to attack Rome. Fortuna was by origin probably a deity of agriculture, where good fortune may play as large a part as hard work; she was accepted in Rome as a goddess of luck.

Above
Flora as goddess of flowering crops was surrounded in the imagination of poets by all that was beautiful. Her attendants in this fresco from Pompeii are the three Graces, daughters of Jupiter, personifications of loveliness, who perhaps were originally goddesses of vegetation. Resting gracefully on each other's shoulders, they hold flowers in their hands. In legends, too, they were fit companions for Venus and rejoiced in such euphonious names as Thaleia, 'flowering', Euphrosyne, 'joy', and Aglaia, 'radiant'.

Right
The Capitol as it appears today. Few visitors to Rome fail to make the pilgrimage up the sloping ramp to the glorious piazza of Michelangelo that now covers both the citadel and the religious centre of the ancient city. Guarding the ramp are two huge statues of Castor and Pollux from the Theatre of Pompey, reminders of their role in Rome's mythology. The modern buildings around the piazza cover the Tabularium, the former public record office, and the Temple of Jupiter, Juno and Minerva, and house a valuable collection of *objets d'art* from Rome's past. Against the balustrade of the Senatorial Palace (rear) two river gods, the Nile and the Tiber, frame a small statue personifying Rome.

THE ESTABLISH-MENT

CHAPTER IV

rcial
pply
after
the
d.

Jupiter was the god of sky and weather and the Ides of each month were set aside for his worship. On that day Jupiter's priest, the Flamen Dialis, would lead a white ewe lamb along the Via Sacra up to the Capitoline Hill and sacrifice it in front of his temple. As a sky god, Jupiter had agricultural interests, which included the inauguration of the Vinalia, or feast of wine on 19th August. Another festival, on 23rd December, celebrated the recovery of light from the darkness of winter solstice. Jupiter shared a vast temple on the Capital with Juno and Minerva, both females. Here the influence of Greek myths played havoc with native Italian traditions, where it is highly doubtful if Jupiter had any connection with either lady. In the course of time, however, Jupiter was identified with the Greek Zeus, Juno with his wife Hera, and Minerva with Athene his daughter, patroness of craftsmen. *Far right* the marriage of Jupiter and Juno is shown in a detail of a Fresco found at Pompeii.

Right

Juno was worshipped under many titles, among them Sospita, Lucina, Sororia, Iuga, Mater Regina, all showing her concern for women in various stages of their lives, as preserver, goddess of childbirth, puberty, and marriage, and queen mother. She played a part in many Roman myths, and it was she who did all in her power to prevent Aeneas's voyage from Troy to Italy. Livy tells us that her worship was brought from the Etruscan city of Veii to Rome in 396 BC. This queenly statue of the goddess is now in the Vatican.

Above

Minerva was the other goddess who with Juno shared the temple of Jupiter Optimus Maximus on the Capitol at Rome. According to tradition the Palladium, her sacred effigy, was brought from Troy to Italy by Aeneas and kept by later generations in the Temple of Vesta, an essential security for the welfare of Rome. In later times she was honoured at the five-day March festival called Quinquatrus. This originally had nothing to do with her — a good example of the way in which confusion arose among the Romans over half-understood traditions and anniversaries. This head of Minerva is from a theatre in Turkey.

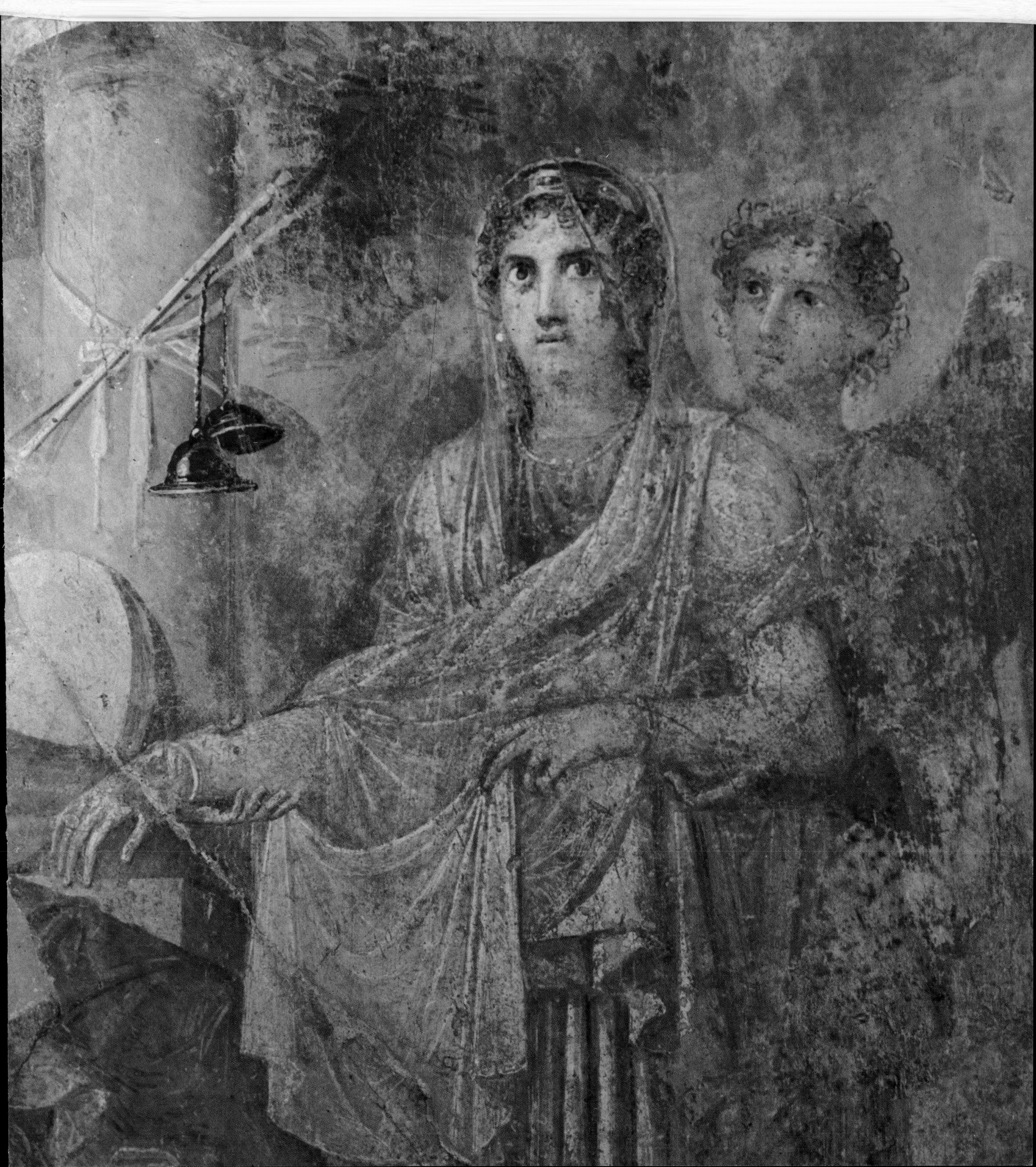

Left
From the foam of this bay near Paphos in Cyprus, according to one legend, Venus sprang, fully formed. When she came to land she took refuge in the myrtle trees, which have been sacred to her ever since. Her worship was popular throughout the island, which points to the Eastern origin of her cult. Thanks to Greek influence, it spread to Sicily, where an important temple was built to her on Mount Eryx. During the early wars against Carthage the Romans gained control of Sicily, and after a consultation of the Sibylline Books, built a temple in Rome to Venus Erucina, which was dedicated in 215 BC.

Below
Stories about Venus, confused with those about the Greek Aphrodite, figure largely in the poems of Ovid. Inevitably the prostitutes of Rome adopted Venus as their cult figure, and honoured her with a festival on 23rd April, a date that was also that of the Vinalia, a wine festival honouring Jupiter. This statuette of Venus in painted marble is from Pompeii, where the goddess was recognized by the citizens as their official protectress.

Right
Romans traditionally derived their descent from Venus through Aeneas and from Mars through Romulus, a link that was perhaps not fortunate — for Mars was traditionally the paramour of Venus, although neither remained exclusively devoted to the other. In this fresco at Pompeii Cupid watches Mars and Venus. To the Romans Mars was certainly a god of war — and therefore the horse was sacred to him as a necessary aid in warfare. Mars also had agricultural functions, and the Roman calendar originally started with his month, March, while his principal festivals were celebrated in the spring, clear indications of his importance to farmers.

Following pages
The allegorical *Birth of Venus* by Botticelli is deservedly one of the most famous paintings of the Renaissance. Venus is the Roman name for the Greek goddess of love, Aphrodite. She played an important role in Roman myth as the mother of Aeneas, founder of the Roman race and ancestor of the Caesars. It is surprising that her worship was not important at Rome until the times of the Caesars. Naturally Julius made her temple the centrepiece of his Forum and gave her the appropriate title of Genetrix — mother. An imposing temple was dedicated to Venus and Rome jointly by the Emperor Hadrian in 135 AD, symbolically underlining their association.

Apollo was a Greek god who did not even change his name when he came to Rome. He was widely worshipped in the Greek-speaking world, and it is not surprising to find abundant evidence of his cult in Italy before the Romans became supreme, especially among the Etruscans. The terracotta statue is in the Villa Giulia, the Etruscan museum in Rome, and is one of several such cult statues from various parts of Etruria. Apollo is often shown as a handsome young man with rather soft features and a splendid head of hair. His oracle at Delphi in Greece, Livy tells us, was often consulted by the Etruscan kings.

Right
Augustus had a particular devotion to Apollo and built him a temple on the Palatine next to his own home, on this site, later occupied by the Stadium of Domitian. The temple was one of the most magnificent in Rome, and beneath its great statue of the god were stored the prophecies which replaced the original Sibylline Books destroyed in the Civil Wars between Marius and Sulla. The Centenary Games held by Augustus in 17 BC were, unusually, dedicated to Apollo, and the poet Horace was commissioned to write a hymn – which

has survived – to be sung by a choir of boys and girls from noble families in honour of the god and his sister Diana. From this time onwards Apollo's cult practically rivalled that of Jupiter.

Below
Temples to Apollo were common throughout Italy. This temple in Pompeii was built in the reign of Nero, shortly before the destruction of the city in 79 AD. It was on the site of a temple of

Diana, originally a goddess of forests, was often portrayed as a huntress, as in this statue. In early Italian history she had been the principal deity of the Latin League, a free association of tribes and cities in central Italy. Her shrine was a sacred grove near Aricia and the modern village of Nemi, a few miles southeast of Rome. Even before Rome became head of the League, a place was found for Diana among the city's deities and a temple was built to her on the Aventine. According to Livy, her worship was established by King Servius Tullius, and its adherents practised a Greek ritual.

pre-Roman times and testities to the active influence of the Greeks in Southern Italy. Games, too, were held annually at Rome in Apollo's honour, a tradition originating from the Second Punic War. These games were characterized by dramatic performances in the Greek manner and combats of gladiators, a native Italian tradition. These were also popular in Pompeii, where there was a large amphitheatre for their display, one of the oldest known.

Below
If Livy is right that Diana's earliest worshippers in Rome practised a Greek ritual, then the way was open to identify her with the Greek Artemis, sister of Apollo, also a goddess of hunting. Both Diana and Artemis helped women by giving them children too, so it was not a big step to portray Diana as a fertility goddess. Here she is portrayed in a cult statue from Ephesus which unashamedly reveals this function.

Left
The Romans evolved no theories of their own about life after death but borrowed their beliefs first from the Etruscans and later from the Greeks. Abundant Etruscan evidence is to be found in the decorations of tombs excavated by archaeologists, a source of wonder even today. This detail of a fresco from a tomb at Tarquinii depicts Hades or Dis, as the Romans called him, king of the Underworld. He wears a wolf's head, to symbolize his omnivorous nature. The name Dis, like another Greek name for him, Pluto, means wealthy, showing the earth both as giver of wealth and receiver of an endless succession of the dead.

Below
Vulcan was the god of volcanic eruptions, well-known in Italy and Sicily from his periodic displays on Vesuvius and Etna. At his festival on 23rd August fish were fried alive, victims which would normally be safe in the sea from the god's power. He was identified with Hephaestus the Greek smith god who lived and worked beneath volcanos. In this picture by Ercole de Roberti, a sixteenth-century Ferra artist, he forges armour on his anvil with the aid of his assistants, the one-eyed Cyclopes. The two suits hanging above the workers' heads may perhaps be intended for Romulus and Remus, shown at right as infants still.

Right
As the patron of *mercatores* – merchants – Mercury made a comparatively late appearance on the Roman scene in 495 BC, when a temple was dedicated to him. The earlier Romans had been active in agriculture rather than in trade, and no doubt felt little need of such protection. Mercury was also Jupiter's messenger and portrayed with conveniently winged feet, as in this statue, in the Naples Museum. He had the same attributes as the Greek god Hermes, who was also worshipped by traders. Horace fancifully saw in the Emperor Augustus an incarnation of Mercury, young and engaging, the god of peaceful arts, restorer of economic prosperity to a world torn apart by civil war.

Above

This majestic figure of Ceres has ears of corn in her hand, symbol of her authority over agriculture. Her first temple at Rome was dedicated after a famine in 496 BC. The goddess, apparently, was imported from Cumae, one of Rome's main corn suppliers at that time. Her annual festival — the Cerealia — was held for eight days from 12th April. On its last day foxes were let loose at the foot of the Aventine Hill, where Ceres's temple stood, with burning brands tied to their tails. Ovid suggests that this commemorated an occasion when a fox caught stealing hens was wrapped in straw to be burnt, then escaped, burning the crops it ran through. Scholars are much tested to explain that one!

Above right

The Romans portrayed their gods as men, so it was a small, albeit a significant, step to regard certain men as divine. There were precedents for this: Aeneas and Romulus each had a divine parent, and more recently Alexander the Great had been venerated as a god among the Greeks. Small wonder that the Romans felt that Julius Caesar's tremendous achievements warranted his apotheosis after death. As Julius's adopted son, Augustus claimed to be *divi filius* — son of the divine — and after his death full divine honours were paid to him and a college of priests was established to maintain his worship. This became the custom with all but the most unpopular emperors. In this statue from the Vatican the Emperor Claudius is portrayed with

the eagle, symbol of Jupiter and Rome, wearing a chaplet of oak leaves, in an act of worship — a man and yet a god.

Right

The cult of Dionysus, latinized as Bacchus arrived in Rome shortly after that of Cybele (see page 60) and although proscribed by the Senate, remained popular. The God is usually shown as the youthful god of wine and good living and there are many representations of the Bacchantes and their orgiastic rituals involving large quantities of wine. Women in particular seemed to indulge in the crazy, drunken worship.

Right

Neptune was originally a not very important god of fresh water, who had nothing to do with salt water until the Romans identified him with the Greek Poseidon. The Romans themselves had little love of the sea, and avoided it wherever possible — witness the fact of the splendid road system throughout the Empire. Neptune's feast day was in midsummer on 23rd July, when streams were low and water scarce, a natural time for countrymen to appeal to a god of fresh water. His cult partner was Salacia, goddess of springing (*salire*) water. Once Neptune became identified with Poseidon, Roman poets assigned him the Greek god's adventures, and this mosaic from Tunisia also shows him in his Greek disguise.

Below

The process of deification was sometimes carried beyond the bounds of credulity. Antinous was the young favourite of the Emperor Hadrian, a rather melancholy and lonely man, as some of his surviving poetry shows. When his beloved Antinous was drowned in Egypt, Hadrian built a city and temples in his honour. Statues, set up elsewhere, emphasized his youth and beauty, as here, where the youth is portrayed as Bacchus with grapes in his hand and a carelessly worn leopard skin.

Right

This second-century temple to Hadrian at Ephesus is situated in a prominent part of the town, like many such temples built in honour of divine rulers throughout the Roman Empire. It was a matter of local pride to put up a worthy building and also a social honour to be elected to the college of priests who serviced it. There were commonly 15 priests, presided over by an ex-magistrate, and ceremonies were held on important anniversaries connected with the emperor concerned. All costs were borne locally, one of the reasons why Boudicca destroyed Colchester in the rebellion she led in East Anglia — Colchester was the site of a temple to Claudius.

THE LEGENDS

CHAPTER

V

Previous page
Daphne, dedicated to virginity,
successfully resisted the advances of all
her suitors, although Peneus felt she
owed him grandchildren. When she met
Apollo, her beauty proved too much for
that amorous god. She fled in terror from
his embraces and begged her father to
save her from Apollo's attentions by
destroying her beauty. She was
transformed on the spot into a laurel tree.
Symbolizing her perpetual youth, the
laurel is an evergreen, and ever after
Apollo's brow was adorned with laurel
leaves. Bernini has cleverly portrayed the
moment of Daphne's transformation in
this composition, which is now in Rome's
Borghese Gallery.

Right
Ovid's stories of Jupiter's amorous
escapades were a source of constant
amusement to his contemporaries,
particularly as the poet himself lived no
cloistered life. One illustrated in this
mosaic from a Cyprus villa built in the
third century AD involved Ganymede, a
pretty young shepherd of Troy. In order
to carry Ganymede off to serve him as a
cup-bearer — and as a constant irritation
to Juno — Jupiter turned himself into an
eagle, his own royal symbol. Other
metamorphoses credited to the god are
those of a fly, a swan, a bull and a shower
of gold.

Right
Among Ovid's many poems, none is more
charming than the 15 books of the
Metamorphoses, or Transformations.
In these books, legendary Greek and
Roman heroes and heroines are
transformed into various shapes and
beings. One of Ovid's stories is that of the
nymph Daphne, illustrated here with her
father, the river god Peneus, in a mosaic
pavement. Apollo had boasted that his
hunting arrows were of more use than
those of Cupid, which played havoc with
people's affections. Cupid in anger shot
Apollo with an arrow of passion and
wounded Daphne, innocent victim, with
another arrow which drove away all
sexual desire.

Far right
Galatea, sea nymph and daughter of
Nereus, a lesser god of the sea, lived off
the coast of Sicily. As depicted here she
attracted the attention of Polyphemus,
one of the mythical one-eyed giants called
the Cyclopes. Descendants of the original
Sky and Earth, the Cyclopes were
portrayed both as shepherds, like
Polyphemus in this picture, and as
blacksmiths at work in their forge under
Mount Etna making thunderbolts for
Jupiter. In the local legend the uncouth
giant Polyphemus, in love with Galatea
but rejected by her, transformed her
handsome young lover Acis into a river
by crushing him with a rock. The story,
told by Ovid, is also the theme of one of
Handel's operas.

Right
Many of the myths of Jupiter, which are largely those of the Greek Zeus, are preserved by Ovid. His *Fasti* tells how the constellation Capricorn got its name. As a baby on the island of Crete Jupiter was suckled along with Pan by a goat from the herd of a mountain nymph. The name Amalthea has been given variously both to the nymph and the goat. When one of the goat's horns fell off it was filled with fruit as a cornucopia, or horn of plenty, and presented to Jupiter by the nymph. The goat – *capra* – and the horn – *cornu* – were translated into stars. The same myth is depicted by Bernini in this small group from the Bernini Gallery.

Below
Narcissus was a handsome young man whose love for himself has immortalized his name in the textbooks of psychologists. One of his lovers prayed that as a punishment for his conceit and frigid disregard of those who loved him, Narcissus would fall desperately in love with someone unable to return his passion. When Narcissus saw his own reflection in a pool, as depicted in this mosaic, he fell so hopelessly in love with himself that he died of grief when his beloved appeared to avoid him. On his death he was transformed into the flower which bears his name.

Right
Ovid tells us that Medusa, a Gorgon, was once renowned for her beauty and roused jealous hopes in the hearts of many suitors. Most striking was her lovely hair. After Neptune seduced her in the Temple of Minerva, the goddess punished Medusa for her impiety by turning her hair into snakes. This is how Medusa is portrayed in this relief. She was slain by Perseus, who used her head to turn to stone all who looked at it. This magic talisman was worn as an effigy on Minerva's breastplate, and was a common feature on armour worn by Roman emperors.

THE IMPORTS

CHAPTER
VI

Previous pages
The Romans usually tolerated and adapted foreign cults unless they were antisocial or subversive. Druidism, for example, was brutally put down in Britain and Gaul because its priests practised human sacrifice and encouraged rebellion against Roman power. Tolerance came from many years of experience and mistakes in Italy before they extended their empire. The worship of Magna Mater, the Great Mother, was frowned on at first by the Senate until it was seen to fulfil a spiritual, not a harmful, purpose. This tolerant attitude is illustrated by these statues of Neptune and Ceres at Smyrna in Turkey, which recall an unsavoury old myth of Neptune's seduction of Ceres, his sister.

Above
Cybele, the Great Mother, was a fertility goddess whose cult originated in Phrygia. It was traditionally brought to Rome in 204 BC, Livy tells us, at a critical point in the Second Punic War, following the advice given by the Sibylline Books. The ship bringing Cybele's statue from Phrygia stuck in the Tiber mud, but the sacred stone was passed from hand to hand by the women of Rome until it came to rest in the Temple of Victory on the Palatine. Cybele's male attendants were eunuchs and her worship was wild and orgiastic. Her annual festival, the Megalesia, on 4th April was strictly controlled by the puritanical Senate, who forbade Roman citizens to take part. This headless statue of the goddess, at Corinth, is a Roman work of the second century AD.

Above right
When the plague broke out in 293 BC, the Sibylline Books were consulted, before the embassy was sent to Delphi, and finally to Epidaurus. Here their reception was mixed. But Aesculapius appeared to one of their envoys in a dream and promised to come next day as a snake. This was a common epiphany of the god, as shown in this small Roman statue from a villa in Cyprus, where he holds a staff with a snake twined round it. The snake is phallic in appearance and therefore a symbol of life, and its venom also has medicinal qualities which were not unknown to the ancients.

The staff entwined by a snake is still the emblem commonly used by doctors to denote their profession.

Right
The sacred snake of Aesculapius obligingly boarded the ship which took the Roman embassy home from Epidaurus. As the ship was coming up the Tiber it slipped overboard and swam to the island which stands in midstream. Here a shrine was erected in Aesculapius's honour and this became a sanatorium, conveniently cut off by the water from the rest of the city. There is still a hospital here and a church, both dedicated to St Bartholomew, who has usurped the god's functions.

Left

The gods of Egypt were welcomed in Rome chiefly by the poorer classes, who probably enjoyed some of the more unsavoury aspects of their worship and the continual round of ritual, which was foreign to Roman ideas. The best-known gods were Isis and Osiris, rulers of the Underworld, the one representing the female reproductive force of nature, the other a legendary king murdered by his brother. When Egypt came under the control of Alexander the Great, his general Ptolemy introduced the god Serapis as a combination of Osiris and the Greek gods Zeus, Hades and Asclepius. Serapis was never popular with the Egyptians, but he was worshipped throughout the Roman Empire. This bust of him was found at the Roman colony of Carthage.

Below left

Ovid in his *Metamorphoses* tells how Aesculapius came to Rome. His name is a Latinized corruption of Asclepius, the legendary son of Apollo, patron of physicians, whom he helped by visiting the sick in their dreams. Centres of pilgrimage were to be found throughout the Greek-speaking world and the sick flocked to them in hopes of a cure. They spent their time lying on stretchers in the long colonnades which are a feature of such sanctuaries — this one is at Pergamum in Turkey. The most famous centre was at Epidaurus in Greece, where a Roman embassy came in 293 BC to ask Aesculapius to cure a pestilence that was raging in Rome.

Top right

Mithras was a god from Persia, and his first missionaries in the West were some pirates spared by Pompey the Great who settled in Italy. The religion was also spread by Roman troops who had served in the Eastern Mediterranean, and it always remained popular with soldiers. Unfortunately our knowledge of Mithraism is limited to what its opponents tell us and the interpretation of symbols never meant to be intelligible to outsiders. Mithras was apparently born from a rock and after various adventures caught and tamed a supernatural beast represented in sculpture as a large bull, which he afterwards sacrificed. This act is as central to Mithraism as the Crucifixion is to Christianity. This sculpture, now in the Vatican Museum, portrays the moment of sacrifice.

Right

Mithras was often identified with the sun and one of his commonest titles was Sol Invictus — the Unconquered Sun. His birthday fell on 25th December, so our Christmas has a Mithraic origin. In a meeting place such as this underground chamber, found under the Church of St Clement in Rome, devotees of Mithras underwent a series of seven grades of initiations which tested their courage and determination. A life of purity was the aim because Mithras stood for the triumph of good over evil.

Previous pages
The Villa of the Mysteries at Pompeii
takes its name from the vivid series of
frescos in one of its rooms. An air of
religious mystery surrounds them, and
the various scenes have caused much
scholarly controversy. The central fresco
depicts the wedding of Bacchus and
Ariadne, presumably to symbolize the
physical bliss and mental satisfaction
which follow an initiation. Here a young
woman kneels with her head on an older
matron's lap while she is scourged,
perhaps to expiate the faults of her
previous life. The other scenes bear out
the interpretation that this is a Bacchic
mystery rite, which became so popular
in Italy as to be banned by decree of the
Senate in 186 BC.

ΠΟΛΥΜΝΙΑ ΕΥΤΕΡΠΕΙ ΘΑΛΕΙΑ ΟΥΡΑΝΙΑ

THE SOURCES

CHAPTER VII

Traditional sources of poetic inspiration
were the nine Muses, here painted by the
Sienese artist Baldassarre Peruzzi as
attractive young women dancing with
their patron and protector, Apollo. Their
favourite mountain retreat was Parnassus,
high above Delphi in Greece, site of
Apollo's ancient oracle. Each Muse was
responsible for a particular branch of the
arts — Melpomene for tragedy, Calliope
for epic, *inter alias.* Virgil opens his
Aeneid with an invocation to one of
them, a ritual copied from earlier Greek
epic poets, and Ovid frequently mentions
his need of their help. Even Livy ends the
preface to his *History* with an appeal for
divine assistance, which shows that Livy
saw himself as a poet.

Left

In this mosaic portrait of Virgil, found in 1896 at Sousse in Tunisia, the poet is seated between two Muses, Melpomene clearly identified by the tragic mask in her hand, Clio, patroness of history, by the open scroll. The *Aeneid* on his knee is open at the words *Musa, mihi causas memora* – 'Muse, relate to me the reasons'.

Virgil died in his early fifties and was buried at Naples, where his tomb was revered in later ages. There is even a legend that St Paul wept at his grave. In his will Virgil directed that the *Aeneid* should be destroyed because it was imperfect. The Emperor Augustus fortunately prevented this, instructing the editors to correct and remove redundant passages but add nothing. The epitaph on Virgil's tomb contains his whole career in eleven Latin words:

Mantua gave me life, Calabria death –
    I lie
In Naples – poet of herdsmen, farms
    and heroes

Below left

Ovid was born in the Abruzzi, a mountainous region east of Rome whose isolation has only recently been penetrated by roads. Sulmona was Ovid's home town – *Sulmo mihi patria est* – a Latin phrase whose initial letters S M P E are now Sulmona's municipal motto. He came from a well-to-do but obscure family and was destined by education in Rome for a political career. But this proved uncongenial. In Pope's famous rendering, 'I lisped in numbers and the numbers came'; poetry was to be Ovid's life and he moved in a brilliant literary circle where he found much to his liking. This small town set high among the Apennines is typical of many in the district from which the poet came.

Below

In his fifties Ovid was banished from Rome to a barbaric frontier post, Tomi, later Constanza, in Rumania. The reasons are obscure, but his name was linked with that of Julia, the Emperor Augustus'

daughter, who had been banished earlier. From Tomi Ovid poured out a series of poems lamenting his fate, but to no avail. The decree was never revoked, and he died in exile. The modern Constanza seems a pleasant place, and the Black Sea coast has become a popular tourist centre. But it was apparently very different in Ovid's day, and he never ceased to complain of the climate and his surroundings. This statue of him was erected at Constanza in 1879.

Above
Ovid wrote a quantity of poems, all with a light touch, the majority in a racy and humorous vein. One poem in 15 books of hexameter verse is the *Metamorphoses*, a rich store of mythology from the creation of the world to the death of Julius Caesar. The stories' common theme is, of course, a change of shape. One such tale is that of Venus's love for the handsome Adonis, the subject of this voluptuous painting by Veronese, now in the Prado in Madrid. Ovid describes Adonis lying under a poplar tree with his head resting on Venus's breasts while she warned him about the dangers of hunting. He neglected her warning and was killed by a wild boar — and anemones sprang up where his blood had sprinkled the ground.

ΘΙСΒΗ

ΠΥ ΡΑΜΟС

Above
Ovid's *Metamorphoses* has been used by
writers as well as artists as a dictionary of
mythology. Shakespeare read the poem
at school and remembered many of the
stories:

> In such a night
> Did Thisbe fearfully o'ertrip the dew,
> And saw the lion's shadow ere himself,
> And ran dismay'd away.

Jessica reminds Lorenzo in *The Merchant
of Venice*. Pyramus and Thisbe, shown
here in a mosaic from Cyprus, are also
familiar from the brilliant and humorous
scenes in *A Midsummer Night's Dream*,
while Venus and Adonis are the subjects
of a poem nearly 1200 lines long. The
other work of Ovid's mature years is the
Fasti, the Calendar. It is an account of
the festivals in the Roman religious year,
enlivened by much mythology. These
two poems have provided much of the
material for this book.

Left
Livy was born at Patavium in Northern
Italy, which is now the flourishing
modern city of Padua, seen here. He
never lost his *patavinitas*, a feature of his
Latin not always approved of by his
contemporaries, and his bourgeois
background is reflected in his detachment

from the political struggles of his time.
His history of Rome from its foundation
to his own day comprised 142 books,
most of which have been lost. Enough
survives to appreciate the value of Livy's
work, and some of his material has been
used here to relate the stories of early
Rome. Unashamedly patriotic, even in
the face of facts, Livy sees this early
period as the reason for Rome's
greatness in his own time. He may
not measure up to what we expect of
a historian today, but as a storyteller
he is unforgettable.

Right
The Golden Age of Latin literature, when
Livy, Ovid and Virgil were all writing, was
presided over by the Emperor Augustus,
here shown in Olympian pose with an
infant Rome at his feet. This flowering of
literature was no accident but the result
of Augustus' deliberate policy, and carried
out by his friend Maecenas, who gathered
around him a circle of writers. In days
when the sale of books was no means of
livelihood, patronage was a professional
writer's only hope. Certainly Augustus
took a close personal interest in literature
— we are told that Virgil read many
passages of the *Aeneid* to him. So the
patriotic sentiments should hardly
surprise us.

14
MVNIF. PI. IX. P. M.
AN. XVIII

On Mount Parnassus, Apollo, patron of the arts, sits under the laurel trees sacred to him, playing his lyre. He is surrounded by the figures of all nine Muses and many writers, prominent among them the three great poets of Greek, Latin and Italian literature, Homer, Virgil and Dante, who stand on the left of Apollo. This delightful combination of fact and fancy was painted by Raphael as one of a series of frescoes in the Vatican. Perhaps better than any other, this picture summarizes the influence of classical mythology and of the writers who have made it a tradition that is still living today.

ACKNOWLEDGEMENTS

The publishers would like to thank the following individuals and organizations for their kind permission to reproduce the pictures in this book:

Alinari 58 left
F C Birch, Sonia Halliday Photographs Ltd 32 bottom
C A Bulland 20
Capitoline Museum, Rome 22 bottom, 26 bottom
Elek Books Ltd 40, 43, 44 bottom, 45
B Facchinelli & Co 70 bottom
Italian Tourist Office 68 bottom left
Michael Holford 18 below, 23 left, 27 top, 33 bottom
Octopus Books Ltd 12 bottom, 14-16, 18-19
J Powell 38 bottom
Roumanian Tourist Office 68 right
Scala 8-9, 11, 13, 17, 21, 22 top, 24-5, 27 bottom, 28-9,
    30 bottom, 32 top, 33 top, 34 top, 39, 41, 42 right,
    46-7, 48-9, 50-2, 54 left, 55, 57, 58 top, 61, 63-7,
    69, 71-2
Sonia Halliday Photographs Ltd endpapers, 5, 7, 10, 12 top,
    23 right, 26 top, 30 top, 31, 35, 38 top, 42 left, 44 top,
    49, 54, 56, 58 right, 59-60, 62, 68 top, 70 top
Spectrum Colour Library 44 top, 50 bottom left, 53